Motorcycle combinations of the Federation of Sidecar Clubs gathered in the sidecar paddock at the British Motorcycle Federation show at Peterborough in May 1993. In the foreground, from left to right, are a Watsonian Palma and a racy-looking home-made sports sidecar. The three immediately behind these two are, from left to right, another Palma, a Hedingham Sports and a Squire QM1 saloon, all modern touring outfits.

SIDECARS

Jo Axon

Shire Publications Ltd

CONTENTS

Published by Shire Publications Ltd, Midland House, West Way, Botley, Oxford OX2 0PH. Copyright © 1997 by Jo Axon. First published 1997; reprinted 2007. Transferred to digital print on demand 2011. Shire Library 332. ISBN 978 0 74780 344 7.

Jo Axon is hereby identified as the author of this work in accordance with Section 77 of the Copyright, Designs and Patents Act 1988.

All rights reserved. No part of this publication may be reproduced or transmitted in any form or by any means, electronic or mechanical, including photocopy, recording, or any information storage and retrieval system, without permission in writing from the publishers.

Printed in Great Britain by PrintOnDemand-Worldwide.com, Peterborough, UK.

British Library Cataloguing in Publication Data. Axon, Jo. Sidecars. – (Shire album; no. 332). 1. Motorcycle sidecars – History. I. Title. 629.2'275'09. ISBN 978 0 74780 344 7.

Editorial Consultant: Michael E. Ware, former Curator of the National Motor Museum, Beaulieu.

ACKNOWLEDGEMENTS
Photographs are acknowledged as follows: Andrew Barber, page 5 (bottom); Mary Blackaby, page 15 (top); Lynn Boom, page 19 (bottom); Steve Boom, page 4; Mr Brightwell, page 21 (top); Tony Bryant, page 29 (centre); Jim and Rose D'Arcy, page 29 (top); Mark Hooper, page 14 (lower); courtesy of the Imperial War Museum, page 7; Toby Miller, page 29 (bottom); Bob Norman, page 11 (top); Keith Walsh, page 23 (bottom); Watsonian Squire, pages 5 (top), 6 (centre), 9, 10 (lower centre), 16 (top), 17 (top), 19 (top), 19 (centre), 20 (bottom); Percy Whellock, page 15 (centre); Roy Workman, pages 2 and 30.

Cover photograph courtesy of Chris Arthur of Watsonian Squire Ltd.

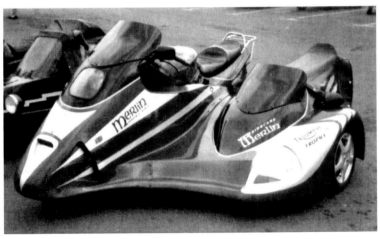

The Merlin F2 Sport was first designed as a track day racing sidecar, but demand from the road touring fraternity has seen refinement to this low-profile moulded sidecar. A faired-in section joining machine and sidecar body is available for both this and the Merlin Super Sport (see page 29). The wide track of the F2 sidecar offers good road-holding stability, aided by adjustable suspension and toe-in facility.

A 1914 wicker sidecar. The same design was used for early invalid Bath chairs. This outfit is the Overseas, manufactured from 1909 to 1915, mainly for export to the colonies, and is now very rare.

FROM THE EARLY DAYS UP TO THE 1920s

Both bicycles and petrol engines existed well before 1900 and it was a logical step to combine the two. Steam power had been used very early on, in the 1860s, but the petrol combustion engine had been introduced by many vehicle manufacturers before 1900. Early motor bicycles were fitted with a single seat, a bicycle-type saddle, but in the 1920s it became possible for a rider to convey a companion by means of a pillion seat pad that could be exchanged for the carrier fitted to the rear mudguard. The earliest known sidecar-type passenger carrier for fitting to a two-wheeled vehicle was produced by an unknown maker for a pedal cycle in 1893. It consisted of a sparse frame supported on one wheel, a saddle and a footrest. A great many motorcycles were produced during the 1890s, and sidecars and sidecarriers designed to accommodate passengers and merchandise appeared in increasing numbers soon after 1900. Trailers, detachable forecars and tricars also appeared, but by 1910 the motorcycle and sidecar combination was clearly the most popular passenger conveyance apart from the car.

One of the first combinations to be marketed was the Montgomery in 1902. Mills & Fulford (later renamed Millford) produced another in 1903, followed by one from Graham Brothers and the Liberty Sociable attachment from the manufacturers of Ariel motorcycles. Other manufacturers soon joined their ranks, including Noxal, Chater-Lea, Matchless, Duco, Veena and Rudge-Whitworth. These early sidecars were of wicker basketwork construction, in the style of Bath chairs used for carrying invalids, set on lightweight chassis with a large wheel. Early sidecars were referred to as 'ladies' attachments', 'pleasure bodies' or 'chairs', and the motorcycle and sidecar together as an 'outfit' or 'combination', although in the United States an outfit is called a 'rig' or a 'plot', terms occasionally used in Britain.

3

Montgomery put a flexibly fitted combination on the market in 1906 but it was soon dropped after owners complained that the outfit was liable to skid on muddy roads and was unstable when stationary. A rigid fitting was eventually established as the most successful method of attaching the sidecar, particularly later when stouter motorcycle frames and chassis prevented fractures of the fine metal tubing.

Other ideas tried and tested were the caster-wheel sidecar, which was unsatisfactory when parking the vehicle, the banking sidecar, which enabled the sidecar wheel to lean in or out on cornering, and duplex steering. This last invention allowed the sidecar wheel and the front motorcycle wheel to turn simultaneously. It proved unpopular for ordinary road use but was later taken up in various motorcycle sports.

There were a number of suspension systems in use: the spring wheel (the sidecar wheel sprung between two leaf springs); coil springs, as used in sprung furniture; cee springs, which were large C-shaped springs attached between the sidecar body and the chassis, usually set at the rear but sometimes front and rear; and elliptical springs, each designed as half a leaf spring, and two of which would be fitted usually at the rear of the sidecar body instead of cee springs. All these forms of suspension gave an extremely bouncy ride; eventually a restricting damper was added to control the violent springing action.

By 1910 a large number of motorcycle manufacturers were producing complete combinations, and many other firms marketed sidecars only. It was soon realised that sidecars provided a cheaper form of motorised vehicle than four-wheeled vans or trucks, and almost every trade used the motorcycle combination, including carpenters, window-cleaners, chimney-sweeps, pharmacists, butchers, milkmen, photographers and blacksmiths. Sidecarriers were even used for transporting small farm animals, such as pigs, sheep and calves.

The Watsonian sidecar business was started by Fred Watson at his small house in Birmingham in 1911. He originally named his family firm the Patent Collapsible Sidecar Company, after his box-type sidecar and chassis, which folded to a width of 2 feet 8 inches (81 cm), allowing the whole outfit to pass down the narrow

The 1912 Wilkinson combination. The coachbuilt sidecar has a small entry door, a car-type upright screen and a pram-type pull-over hood for wet weather. The sidecar wheel is surprisingly small for an early model; at this period most were the motorcycle size of 19 inches (48 cm) or more.

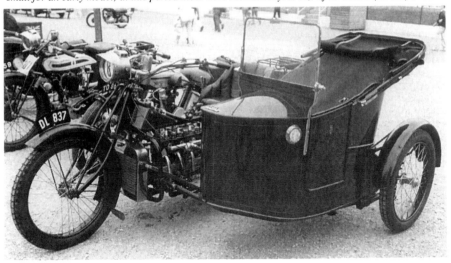

A Watsonian trade sidecarrier advertising their Folding Sidecar Company in 1912. Note the cee springs at the front and rear of the chassis.

passage next to his house without the sidecar being detached. In those days few modest homes were built with the luxury of a driveway; in many cases the only access to the rear of the house was a footpath about 36 inches (91 cm) wide. In 1912 the firm was renamed the Watsonian Folding Sidecar Company Limited, and by 1914 they were advertising a large number of standard models. As the sales potential was realised, other makers marketed similar folding chassis, among them the Dorway and the Paragon. The sidecar body had first to be removed, complete with frame and leaf springs, then the wheel could be pushed to fold the chassis up

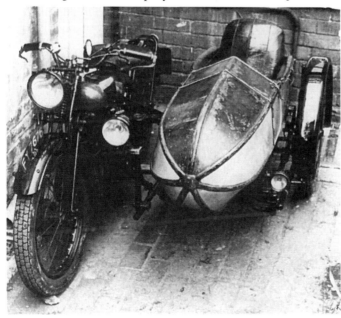

The Dorway folding chassis sidecar of the 1920s. When the body was removed the chassis could be folded up against the motorcycle by pushing on the wheel.

5

Triumph Motorcycles' Gloria sports sidecar of 1922, fitted on cee springs under the front and full leaf springs under the rear.

Watsonian's Light Sporting sidecar, 1920s. The torpedo or cigar shape was produced by many firms at this time for speed racing events. This model had front coil springs and rear cee springs.

A 1920s racing-style Norton sidecar of torpedo shape.

The 24th Battalion Motor Machine Gunners with Clyno outfits awaiting inspection by General Horne at Dieval, 12th June 1918. These sidecars were little more than chassis fitted with a platform to support the armoury.

against the motorcycle, reducing the vehicle's width to 28 inches (71 cm).

In 1914 A. J. Stevens (AJS Motorcycles) made two sidecar-wheel-drive combinations for himself and one of his sons, but two-wheel-drive outfits did not find favour until the late 1930s. AJS sidecars were later marketed under the trade name of Graiseley, and Triumph motorcycles marketed theirs as Gloria sidecars. For racing, standard single-seat sidecars were coupled to machines, but by the 1920s participants required more specialised vehicles and cigar-shaped sports bodies were favoured. Among the suppliers of these were Hughes, Swallow, Watsonian, Helen, Norton and Noxal.

During the First World War sidecars were used for many transport jobs. Vickers Limited, in conjunction with the Clyno Engineering Company and Royal Enfield, issued mobile mounts for the Maxim-type machine-gun for use by the Motor Machine Gun Corps. Many sidecarriers were purpose-built as stretchers and supply boxes by Watsonian. Also in military use were Norton, Mills & Fulford, Rudge, Scott, Sunbeam and BSA combinations. Hendee/

Indian, Harley Davidson and Cleveland combinations were used by the Americans. The Italians had the Frera, and the Germans the NSU military combinations.

Following the First World War a surplus of military vehicles made motorcycles affordable to many of the transport-hungry public. Ex-army motorcycles were easily fitted with a one- or two-seater sidecar to suit the family man's requirements, providing an incentive for further sidecar manufacture.

In the 1920s the General Post Office attached trade boxes to BSA, Hudson, Douglas and Rover motorcycles. Some of these were constructed in wickerwork, but an increasing number were coachbuilt (metal panels over a wooden frame). The Automobile Association (AA) used Chater-Lea combinations and the Royal Automobile Club (RAC) chose Norton. British Merryweather light fire appliance units were fitted on to sidecarriers made by Watsonian, who also provided purpose-built trailers for these outfits. In the 1920s several firms, including Dunelt and Watsonian, produced a convertible sidecar chassis which required less than two

7

minutes to change the tradesman's box for the 'pleasure body'.

William Lyons and a partner started the Swallow Sidecar Company in Blackpool in 1922, specialising in sports sidecars. Within five years the firm had turned to making cars, producing the Austin Swallow in 1927, and the company was renamed the Swallow Sidecar Coachbuilding Company. In 1931 'Sidecar' was dropped from the company's name and later the sidecar side of the business was sold.

Watsonian marketed their Kwik Fit sidecar chassis in 1926. This useful idea allowed the sidecar to be attached and detached quickly. It was advertised that no tools were required for the job, detachment took just twenty seconds, and the sidecar could easily be pushed along a narrow path into the backyard of a house, supported by the addition of the small 'let-down' jockey wheel. Watsonian produced the Kwik Fit chassis for thirty-three years.

Several firms, but principally Watsonian, made juvenile sidecars for pedal cycles, also fitting tandem bicycles, so that a small child could be carried. Most of these small sidecars had flexible fittings (this allowed the bicycle to lean as a solo) and were easily detachable. A number of small trade boxes for bicycles were also available.

A miniature version of the traditional style of single-seat sidecar, this 1930s Watsonian Juvenile cycle sidecar has a removable folding hood. This type was also used for carrying a baby.

THE 1930s AND 1940s

By the late 1930s few sidecar firms were making wickerwork sidecar bodies; instead, they were concentrating on traditional coachbuilding, with the more adventurous using polished aluminium or pressed alloy. The launch-style sidecar body had become popular and remained so into the late 1940s. Design in chassis suspension showed few improvements. Watsonian's flexible wheel chassis (the wheel axle was mounted in rubber) was a similar idea to the swing axle of the German sports Steib. Steib sports sidecars were imported to Britain by AFN of Middlesex in substantial numbers from the mid 1920s until 1938, and from after the Second World War into the 1960s.

Edward Bowser of Leeds produced two Bowser sidecar models in the mid 1930s, the outlines comparable with the later designs of the 1950s. They were the Super Sports and the Streamline saloon, both with a curved nose, sloping boot outline and solid-disc large wheel.

Noxal Sidecars had ceased production before the Second World War but reappeared late in the 1940s under a new trade name, CM Sidecars, an abbreviation of the family firm's name of Connors Motors Limited. Their neat semi-launch-style Hertford of the 1930s was replaced by the pressed alloy sports Airflow and the larger saloon Paramount, the smooth lines showing the influence of aircraft design.

The Garrard S90 sports was the last model to be offered by Bill Garrard before the Second World War began. Its success prompted production into the late 1940s and 1950s of the improved S90 sports and the new Grand Prix sports. This last model was an attempt to copy the sought-after Steib S500L sports sidecar.

After the Swallow Coachbuilding Company dropped the word 'Sidecar' from its name in 1931, Charles Hayward and later Millford supplied chassis for them until 1935. Grindlays of Coventry then continued building Swallow chassis until the outbreak of the Second World War. Late in 1934 Swallow had become a public limited company and in 1945 the sidecar side of the business was sold to the Helliwell Group and became known as the Swallow Coachbuilding Company (1935) Limited. In 1948 the business was sold yet again, to Tube Investments Limited at Walsall Airport, Staffordshire, retaining the Swallow name. Among many other models, the metal Jet 80 sports sidecar was introduced at this time, using rear-mounted rubber torsion suspension. The first models were fitted with a polished wheel disc, with a low screen as optional.

Watsonian officially changed their name in 1931 to the Watsonian Sidecar Company Limited. The number of models increased during the 1930s, as did the demand for commercial and racing sidecars. Their Continental touring sports model, offered late in 1938, was a metal sidecar,

The popular launch-style sidecar favoured by many sidecar producers. This one is a 1936 Watsonian Launch Tourer. The suspension was double coil springs supporting the front and cee springs at the rear of the chassis.

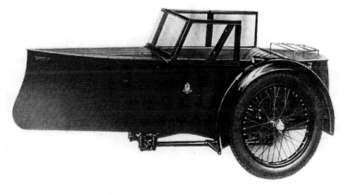

another copy of the German Steib. It was a forerunner of their 1960s fibreglass Grand Prix sports design, but production of the Continental was halted by the hostilities of 1939.

The Brough Superior Black Alpine sports sidecar of the 1930s had a substantial encircling chassis with the front section looped over the sidecar nose; this chassis served as an auxiliary petrol tank, having a Schrader pressure valve placed on the top of the loop over the sidecar. The Alpine sports body was low, sleekly elegant and coachbuilt.

By the 1930s Triumph of Coventry had dropped the trade name Gloria Sidecars and continued under their well-known motorcycle production name with two chunky-looking coachbuilt sports models, the ST and the SS, and the more conventionally styled LT.

In the 1930s Millford sidecars were marketed under the name of the London-based motorcycle dealer Pride & Clarke. Coventry Eagle, a firm known as makers of small two-stroke motorcycles, produced lightweight sports sidecars and a commercial box before the Second World War. The Variable Pitch Sheet Metal Company Limited, a firm involved in the aircraft industry, produced the VP Viper sports sidecar, with a chassis, and a monocoque (chassisless) saloon, the VP Volante. Both were

Top: *The graceful lines of the Noxal Hertford Sports, made during the 1930s. The windscreen was of safety glass, a full hood was supplied and there was ample boot space.*

Upper centre: *The Garrard S90 of the 1930s, with Garrard's chassis loop over the sidecar nose. The boot contained a child's dickey seat.*

Lower centre: *Watsonian's Lilleshall Sports, a coachbuilt lightweight model of the 1930s.*

Bottom: *The Henley, a Watsonian model of the 1930s. The length of the boot area housed a dickey seat, converting it to an occasional two-seater model, and the hood was pulled up in pram style.*

The Norman family's 1936 New Imperial outfit. The sidecar's nose shape became very popular later on, in the 1950s and 1960s.

made in polished light-gauge steel and aluminium alloy, using the stressed skin principal, and produced from 1948 until the mid 1950s. The Viper sports sidecars are seen attached to many earlier motorcycles, but the Volante is now rarely sighted.

The sport of cross-country trialling provided both an ideal testing ground and an invaluable source of publicity for a number of sidecar manufacturers, not only for trials sidecars but also for touring sports models. Among others, Ron Watson of Watsonian and Bill Garrard of Garrard Sidecars frequently competed in person. The earlier trials sidecars remained basically identical to the touring open sports models until the late 1940s, with the same bolted-on chassis and large wheel. Motorcycle scrambling events became more spectacular when sidecars were added in the 1930s and 1940s. These sidecars were also standard touring open sports models, but fitted on to wider chassis than those used in trialling. The road-racing sidecar slowly developed from the standard touring open large-wheel model in the late 1930s to a low kneeling platform with large wheel in the late 1940s, and with the chassis still a bolt-on attachment to the standard motorcycle.

With the start of the Second World War,

The VP Viper Sports sidecar in polished aluminium, made in the late 1940s by the Variable Pitch Sheet Metal Company.

11

A German Zundapp and Steib military combination as used during the Second World War. These sidecars are still being copied by the Russians and many can be seen today in Britain. The name 'Steib' can be seen pressed into the steel side of the nose near the grab handle.

many sidecar firms ceased production or diversified, and those securing ministry contracts stopped making touring sidecars. The Norton Big 4 outfits (with the normal rear-wheel drive plus sidecar-wheel drive) and the purpose-built Ariel combinations, along with many others, played an important role for Britain. The Norton Big 4's two-wheel drive coped admirably in the North African desert. The United States forces made only moderate use of the Harley Davidson and Indian combinations, as the Willys Jeep proved more versatile. Germany made full use of the Zundapp, the NSU outfits and the BMW with Steib sidecar. The BMW and Steib became a two-wheel-drive version by 1940 but this was too costly to produce and was abandoned in 1943 in favour of the standard single-wheel drive.

The Russians were building BMWs under licence until Germany declared war on them, but they continued making outfits with their own M72, a similar machine, and sidecar. The Belgians had the FN and the Gillet, the French the René Gillet, the Sarolea and the Gnome-Rhône model AX2 sidecar-wheel drive. The BMW was also in use in the Netherlands, where the Dutch also had the BSA, and the Sankyo type 97 was employed by the Japanese.

When war ended in 1945, military motorcycles were auctioned off cheaply in massive numbers in Britain, and the addition of a sidecar put family transport within reach of many unable to afford a car. Sidecar businesses grew rapidly during the late 1940s and into the 1950s, and demand for the large coachbuilt saloons almost exceeded that for the sports tourers.

Busmar's Lancastria of 1950, a double-adult coachbuilt saloon sidecar of the type much in demand for family outings.

This home-built road-race kneeler outfit has a Saab engine placed well forward and small wheels all round. It was constructed in 1968.

BOOM AND DECLINE: THE 1950s AND 1960s

The fully enclosed family saloon sidecar had become the most popular model by the early 1950s. Existing sidecar firms and many new ones offered single-seat, double-adult and even four-seater saloons for families, while the demand for commercial sidecarriers had dropped by 1960. The motorcycle sports of racing, trialling and scrambling still required custom-made models, and Garrard, Canterbury and Watsonian were among those who supplied production and custom sidecars for these sports.

Garrard Sidecars of London continued with several larger modified versions of their popular S90 touring sports model and in 1958 brought out their double-adult saloon, the Silver Cloud. It had an unusual side-hinged front, incorporating the front screen and opening in one piece for the passenger to get in, instead of the normal full side door. Their bullet-shaped mono-coque Grand Prix single-seat and child-adult sports were the last models offered by Garrard late in the 1950s. These models continued well into the mid 1960s, when Garrard ended production.

The motorcycle firm OEC from Portsmouth, Hampshire, producers of two-stroke motorcycles in the early 1950s, made sports sidecars with tubular steel frames covered by metal sheeting. Rear

suspension was by plungers in cylindrical casings, with helical springs above and below, and the front of the sidecar body was mounted on rubber pivots.

The German Steib sports sidecars, imported by AFN of Middlesex until the mid 1960s, remained the most popular and stylish of all sports sidecars. A number of other firms modelled their sports sidecars on Steib but could not match their quality.

The Swallow sidecar business produced several saloon sidecars along with their best-selling Jet 80 and Commando sports models until 1956, when they were bought out by Watsonian.

The best-known firms producing a wide choice of saloon models at this time were Blacknell, Busmar, Canterbury, Rankin, Streamline, Surrey and Watsonian.

In the late 1950s Blacknell of Nottingham continued to make their distinctive Bullet single-seat sports sidecar in its encircling chassis. Also available, in sheet-metal panelling, were seven saloon models, ranging from single-seat to spacious double-adult. One of these, the Blacknell Safety saloon, was set within their Safety chassis, which had a raised loop fender across the front of the sidecar nose. Five further coachbuilt sports models were offered before Blacknell ceased manufacture in the mid 1960s. The last was the Biar-

Above: *The neat bullet-shaped German Steib S501 sidecar. The screen was an optional extra, fitting behind the secured weatherproof canvas apron. The flowing line of the mudguard was set off by the stylish top grab handle with integral sidelights.*

Left: *Produced by Phelon & Moore, a 1958 M100 Panther motorcycle and 1959 Panther sidecar chassis. It had lean-out adjustment, an optional carrier for the interchangeable spare wheel, and a support leg on the outer chassis frame, which made jacking up the sidecar an easy operation. In the background is a 1955 Canterbury Warrior sports sidecar.*

ritz, a single-seat lightweight glass-fibre sports sidecar designed for scooters.

Busmar Sidecars of Blackpool began in 1950 by producing a number of large saloon models in light-alloy sheet metal, all with ample headroom and generous length. Eight saloon models were offered, and three sports models. A feature of the Busmar saloon sidecar was the front screen's heavy rubber retaining moulding with rounded corners. Perhaps the most widely and easily recognised Busmar sidecar model is the Astral double-adult, a large oval-shaped saloon, the last saloon model from this prolific firm. Their chassis were robustly constructed and had their own unique Gregoire wheel suspension, a combined spring and damper unit.

Canterbury from Romford, Essex, began in the late 1940s. Three sports sidecars and no less than seventeen saloon models had been produced by the early 1960s, all in sheet-metal panelling. In 1959 the firm brought out their Canterbury Belle, a two-seater boat-cum-sports sidecar, fitted with an 80 cc JAP engine; the body was easily removable from the versatile GMC10a chassis, which had a solid disc wheel. Two more sports models appeared before production ended in the mid 1960s, the Dart and the Arrow. Canterbury saloon sidecars can be identified by the triple ventilator grille set on either side of the sidecar nose.

Right: *Busmar's Astral, a very popular saloon model sold in the early 1960s. Note the heavy retaining rubber moulding around the front screen.*

Below: *The Canterbury Carmobile of 1960, a treble-adult seater, the largest saloon this firm produced. In sheet metal panelling, it had a canvas sunroof and full door, and the triple ventilator (a Canterbury trademark) can be seen on the side below the corner of the windscreen.*

Below: *The single-seat coachbuilt Canterbury Arrow, 1960. This sports sidecar is on a Watsonian VG chassis with rear elliptical springs. It would originally have been on the Canterbury GMC10a chassis with damped suspension, also fitted to the Carmobile.*

Rankin Sidecars traded in Birmingham from the early 1950s until the mid 1960s. They offered sidecar bodies only, coachbuilt in plywood or metal sheeting, to fit Swallow or Watsonian chassis. Seven saloon models, from child-adult to double-adult, were produced and in 1963 the larger New Ashford MK2, a four-seater saloon in resin-bonded plywood, was offered. The double-adult Dalton followed before this firm ceased manufacture.

Streamline Sidecars of Loughton, Essex, manufactured sidecars from the early 1950s until 1959. Initially they offered sidecar bodies only, but then they produced two solid-wheel chassis. Seven saloon models were made; the last was a single-seat saloon named the Rocket, with a full door and large boot space, the tail fins designed as a useful luggage carrier.

Another prolific sidecar producer from the early 1950s until the mid 1960s was Surrey Sidecars from Coulsdon, but very few remain, owing to their fragile fine plywood coachbuilt construction. Seven saloon models were offered, complete with chassis, through the 1950s. The Surrey Syvan, made in 1956, had the appearance of a double-adult saloon but it was a sidecar camper-tent. When it was sold as a sidecar-cum-caravan its solid top canopy could be lifted to provide over 6 feet (2

Watsonian's Cambridge saloon of 1954, with a large sliding door and sunroof, fitted on the damped suspension SV chassis and with the Watsonian Snail mudguard.

metres) of standing room. The sides of canvas and plywood unfolded outwards, while the chassis wheel was on a transverse plane and could be laid flat and the four corner supports put in place. A small hinged table was fitted, and the interior provided space for two-berth accommodation. The last model offered by Surrey Sidecars in the mid 1960s was the monocoque Scout, a single-seat welded metal sports sidecar, finished in plastic fabric, with an integral screen on the rear-hinged scuttle.

By 1950 Watsonian had added several more saloon models to their already extensive range and three more large saloons were available by the mid 1950s. One of them, the double-adult Cambridge, was fitted with a large sliding door. From 1956 Watsonian sidecars became a mixture of coachbuilding and the new reinforced plastic moulding material and their takeover of the Swallow Coachbuilding Company stimulated them to break away from their previous traditional designs. Experiments included the fibreglass double-adult Oxford and the fibreglass Ascot single-seat saloon in 1958,

Although this small lightweight saloon was named the Swallow Sprite, it was made by Watsonian soon after they bought out the Swallow sidecar business in 1956. The Sprite had a lift-up side-hinged canopy and a small access door and was designed mainly for the scooter market.

The sister model to the Sprite was the Swallow Swift Sports sidecar, another coachbuilt lightweight suited to scooters and small-capacity motorcycles.

but these two models were soon discontinued as they were too costly to produce. In the early 1960s six more coachbuilt saloon models were offered, but soon after, in 1962, the range of semi-sports fibre-glass models (which continue to be produced with only slight restyling) began and the coachbuilt saloons were slowly phased out. Watsonian's most popular model, the coachbuilt Avon single-seat sports sidecar, made from 1948 until 1963, was also discontinued in favour of the new fibre-glass sports models. During the late 1950s Watsonian's chassis were updated, elliptical springs being replaced by damped-wheel suspension. By this time all sidecar manufacturers had changed to the damped-wheel improvement.

Pride & Clarke of London, one of the many large motorcycle dealers of the 1950s and 1960s, marketed a number of saloon sidecars under their own name, but these were made by reputable firms such as Rankin and Watsonian.

Above: An early Watsonian Avon sports sidecar on the VG chassis with rear elliptical springs. The side-hinged scuttle, which included the small side door, lifted up and over, allowing easy access. Popular demand kept it in production for over fifteen years, from the late 1940s until 1963.

Right: The Watsonian Monarch of the early 1960s, a large single-seat coachbuilt sports, with a side-hinged scuttle and small entry door. The mudguard for the 1960s had changed to this large pressed-metal faired style.

FIBRE-GLASS MOULDINGS

When compared with today's fibre-glass resin product, the plastic moulding material of the early 1950s lacked pliancy and strength, so articles made of this early reinforced plastic were heavy and its brittleness made it susceptible to stress fractures. Because of high production costs during the 1950s some sidecar models were developed no further than the prototype or produced in very small numbers. As a result a few rare or unique fibre-glass sidecars have survived.

Reinforced plastic was the ideal new material for the road-racing sidecar of the 1950s, being easily moulded to the low-profile streamlined shape required. Watsonian production racing sidecar bodies appeared at every track, and a few custom-made models too.

In 1954 Plastic Motor Bodies of London designed a low streamlined child-adult saloon, the Adventurer coupé model, with limited headroom, a full door and an integral mudguard. This sidecar weighed far more than any existing coachbuilt model of larger proportions and was much more expensive than other child-adult sidecars on the market. Few were made and by 1958 production ceased.

Wessex Sidecars of Somerset were first introduced in fibre-glass in the early 1950s, offering a monocoque single-seat or child-adult sports models, with nose and tail mouldings identical for easy replacement. The firm moved to Dorset in 1963 and, although production had dwindled by the late 1960s, Wessex Sidecars continued.

The Saxony, a single-seat adaptable saloon or sports sidecar, was made by Protective Treatment Industries of London in 1956. The detachable canopy could be removed and stowed neatly inside the identically curving sidecar nose, while the screen remained in place. Production of the Saxony was short, making it an uncommon model.

Probably the largest long-standing producer of all is Watsonian, originally from Birmingham, but based in Gloucestershire since the early 1980s. Their coachbuilt sidecars were renowned for basic good

The Plastic Motor Bodies (PMB) Adventurer coupé was built as a child-adult saloon, but the limited headroom for the front seat and even less for the child's rear seat, together with the high price, depressed sales. A few were made between 1954 and 1958.

Left: *The first Bambini model from Watsonian in 1956, a compact light-weight sports sidecar designed specifically for scooters. Later Bambini models were moulded with an integral screen surround and the sidelight was placed further back above the mudguard.*

Right: *Watsonian's all fibre-glass Oxford double-adult saloon of 1958. Production of the Oxford was short and only a small number were sold. It had a full door, an integral mudguard and a small sunroof opening.*

value and uniform design. Using the new plastic moulding technique, the first Bambini model emerged in 1956. A single-seat lightweight neat sports sidecar with integral mudguard and separate screen, it was intended for the booming scooter market of the 1950s and it proved an unequalled success. The Bambini quickly progressed to a MK1 version with refinements to integral mudguard shaping and an integral screen. Watsonian also produced two short-lived, and now rare, all reinforced plastic models, the single-seat sports Monaco in 1955, and the double-adult Oxford saloon in 1958. The timing of the Oxford was ill chosen, as sidecarrists of the late 1950s were already turning towards the three-

and four-wheeled small cars which were becoming affordable, and an overpriced saloon sidecar, however appealing, had no chance in this market.

By the early 1960s Watsonian were concentrating production on all fibre-glass models, and the numerous coachbuilt sidecars were phased out completely. The Bambini's success was followed by four new sports models, the single-seat Monza, the single-seat Monaco (in a revised form) and the child-adult Palma, these last two with a front-hinged lifting dash. Along with the stylish Grand Prix single-seat sports, these models were made from the early 1960s and are still being produced. After Watsonian bought the Swallow

The Watsonian Palma child-adult sports sidecar was produced in 1963 and is still a popular family model. The body is suspended within the Silk chassis on a damped small wheel and the front-hinged scuttle lifts for access.

Produced in 1956, the fibre-glass Swallow Jet 80 was modelled on the earlier metal Jet 80, first designed in the late 1940s. This model was fitted with an integral screen surround, although the sidecar pictured here has a replacement screen.

sidecar business in 1956 a few models were still sold under the Swallow trade name until the early 1960s. The new Swallow Jet 80 single-seat sports model of 1956, in fibre-glass, was followed by two similar models, the Jet 90 and Jet 100, and lastly by the Swallow Flight. The Swallow Vulcan in 1959 was a double-adult coachbuilt saloon fitted with a moulded fibre-glass hinged canopy top with a small entry door in the lower body.

Although it would have seemed unlikely for Busmar of Blackpool to deviate from their traditional coachbuilding, they did produce a fibre-glass model in 1957. The Busmar Meteor, which made a brief appearance then, was totally unlike any model this conventional firm had ever produced. It was a single-seat low saloon with a lift-up canopy and an extended integral mudguard, rather banana-shaped. Whether because of its style or the cost,

The overall design of the Swallow Flight of the early 1960s was a larger version of the Bambini. The integral screen surround was also used for the later Bambini and the Jet 80.

Clarenden Fairings of Essex offered a single-seat sports and this child-adult model in 1958. The front scuttle was hinged from midway along the nose and lifted complete with the integral screen, and the whole of the top canopy was hinged at the back for access to the child's seat.

this model was short-lived.

Clarenden Fairings turned their hand to two fibre-glass sidecar models (sold in kit form, bodies only), a sports model and a saloon sidecar, in 1958. The single-seat sports had an integral screen and mudguard, as did the child-adult saloon, but the saloon's canopy was in two parts, hinged at the front and at the back. The flooring was of ³/₈ inch (9.5 mm) thick waterproof plywood and the sidecar bodies were designed to fit on to most chassis. Clarenden sidecars were available until early in 1960.

Ray Hawkesford from Birmingham produced a patented sprung chassis from 1956 and in 1961 designed a car-style four-seater saloon sidecar, the over-generously proportioned Hawkon Four. Although realistically priced, this sidecar was not produced for long.

One other large fibre-glass family saloon sidecar briefly came on the market in the early 1960s, the four-seater Buckingham, made by C. L. Taylor from Aylesbury, Buckinghamshire. The sidecar body was designed to fit on the Watsonian small-wheel SV chassis, the George Clarke small-wheel box-section chassis or the Canterbury 16 inch (40 cm) wheel chassis. The body had two centrally hinged full doors for access to front and rear seats, and for children's safety the rear door could be opened only from outside. A limited number of Buckingham sidecars were made over a short period.

The commercial demand had dropped by the late 1950s, but Watsonian produced the Bambox for the RAC, and Mitchenall made the fibre-glass sidecarrier for AA patrolmen.

The Mitchenall fibre-glass AA box sidecarrier, custom-made for the 1950s patrolman; the moulding includes an integral mudguard.

The Briggs Dolphin, a coachbuilt saloon available as a two- or three-seater model. The design was based on the earlier Canterbury saloons.

MODERN TIMES: FROM THE 1970s ONWARDS

There was renewed interest in the touring sidecar in the 1970s, but while the numerous family sidecar pullers of the earlier years, the big British motorcycles, were no longer being produced, the larger-capacity Japanese, Italian and German motorcycles had become widely available. Although these machines were not designed as sidecar haulers, the few British sidecar manufacturers quickly adapted their fitting kits to suit these motorcycle frames. The most popular motorcycles for touring sidecar work have proved to be the 1100 Honda Goldwing, Z1300 Kawasaki, 1100 Yamaha, 850 and 1000 Moto Guzzi and the larger capacity BMWs. The new British Triumphs are also being widely used.

Briggs coachbuilt sidecars were started in 1974 by Harry Briggs from Redditch, Worcestershire. He offered three saloons of varying sizes and two sports single-seat sidecars, based on the style of the 1960s models. They were sold complete with the Briggs chassis on an 8 inch (20 cm) or 10 inch (25 cm) wheel. In the late 1980s Mr Briggs retired and the firm ceased trading because of the small demand for coachbuilt sidecars.

In the same year Peter Rivers-Fletcher of Squire Sidecars, Bidford-on-Avon, Warwickshire, began production of lightweight fibre-glass single-seat sports side-cars to attach to the imported Jawa 350 motorcycles, for the CZ Company in Czechoslovakia. Squire supplied some 1800 of these small Javelin models over a period of three years, ending when the Jawa CZ Company began producing their own sidecars. From then on Squire made a range of seven fibre-glass sports models, all in a streamlined moulding, the three larger models set within an encircling loop chassis. The lightweight CL2 Loadmaster sidecarrier had a rigidly fitted moulded platform on a small wheel. Squire also made trailers specially designed for towing by solo motorcycle or by an outfit. In 1985 the Squire QM1 double-adult fibre-glass saloon was introduced. The overall shape was similar to a reduced-size Reliant Rialto three-wheel car, and it had an outer chassis frame for impact protection and a 10 inch (25 cm) wheel.

An unusual fibre-glass moulded sidecar produced in the mid 1970s was the Serval Sports, a single-seat sidecar made by Lawson Engineering of Luton, Bedfordshire. By the late 1970s it was renamed the LE Sport and the firm had moved to Stansted Mountfitchet, Essex. This sidecar was a low-profile moulding, with a short screen, very large boot area and a 10 inch (25 cm) wheel on Lawson Engineering's own chassis with fitting arms initially made specifically to fit

Kawasaki, Honda and BMW motorcycle frames only. Later this was extended to include most popular machines.

Another streamlined fibre-glass sidecar from the mid 1970s was the Saluki single-seat saloon made by Siderider Hanolean Limited of Norwich. This one was of monocoque design, on a 10 inch (25 cm) wheel set within the body. Also produced by this firm was a lightweight single-seat sports model, the Terrier, on its own chassis, again with a 10 inch wheel. Siderider sidecars ceased production in the mid 1980s.

During 1978 Unit Sidecars from Sible Hedingham, Essex, made a fibre-glass prototype named the Hedingham Sports. This was a large single-seat sports sidecar with ample boot space coupled with a graceful outline. In 1979 Keith Wash, the man responsible for this popular sidecar, began to manufacture leading links for sidecar work for all makes of motorcycle, plus the smaller motorcycle wheels with car rims which improve the handling of all outfits. In 1989, in response to public demand, a larger model was produced, the XL Family Sport Hedingham, a child-adult model with side-by-side seating, and even more stowage space in the outsize boot area. The first Hedingham model was often favoured by classic motorcycle enthusiasts but looks equally well on modern machines.

Martello Sidecars from Canterbury, Kent, first appeared in the early 1980s, built in fibre-glass. There were two saloon models offered, a single-seat and a child-adult size.

Another coachbuilding business, Gemini Sidecars, was started in 1982 by Fred Yates of King's Norton, Birmingham. Three substantial models were produced: the Swan Nose single-seat saloon, the Low Line and the larger High Line four-seater. These were the modern version of the huge Canterbury Carmobiles of the 1950s and 1960s. By 1988 Gemini sidecars were being made to order by Charnwood Restorations of Coalville, Leicestershire.

Neval Motorcycles from North Lincolnshire began production of Regent sidecars in the early 1980s. The models were the Corvette Supreme and Superior saloons,

A futuristic design for the modern motorcycle, the unmistakable wedge shape of Siderider's Saluki, a monocoque child-adult saloon sidecar. The forward-hinged canopy top lifted up but access was still not easy.

The smaller Siderider sidecar, the Terrier sports, on the Siderider small chassis.

Unit Sidecars' Hedingham single-seat sports, the first model from this Essex firm.

23

The Martello child-adult saloon sidecar. Access is gained by lifting the forward-hinged canopy, and this one has a sizable sunroof.

with side-by-side seating to accommodate a child and an adult. They had a forward-hinged canopy top and were designed for the larger-capacity motorcycles, being very substantial on a tubular or a square-section chassis, with the benefit of an encircling front safety rail. Regent sidecars were produced for only a few years.

Wasp Motorcycles from Salisbury, Wiltshire, already well-known for their high-quality forks and suspension products designed for motorcycle sport, produced two fibre-glass sidecar models in 1984, a saloon and a sports sidecar, both of monocoque construction.

Watsonian Sidecars, through the 1970s

Gemini sidecars are spacious and practical and two-, three- and four-seater models are offered. This Highline three- or four-seater has a canvas sunroof and a full door.

Watsonian's Grand Prix sports, produced from the early 1960s, remains unchanged except that by popular demand a large wheel is available, if preferred to the 10 inch (25 cm) wheel, on the Silk chassis, making this continental-style sidecar more acceptable to fit to a classic machine.

and after their move from Birmingham to Blockley in Gloucestershire by 1980, were producing their four touring fibre-glass sports models, the Palma child-adult, the Monaco single-seat, the Monza single-seat and the Grand Prix single-seat sidecars, unchanged since their first appearance in the early 1960s, and all on the 10 inch (25 cm) wheel. In 1984 Watsonian introduced two more models, the three-seater Oxford and the double-adult Cambridge, both larger sports sidecars on the same lines as the original Palma, also on the small wheel, but wider and with a restyled flat top to the sidecar nose to compliment the Watsonian badge trim.

In 1988 the Squire business merged with Watsonian in Gloucestershire and they became Watsonian Squire Limited. The Squire QM1 saloon was discontinued soon after, as was the small Swallow Gem sports sidecar, but all other models are still produced. In 1995 there was the option of a wider version of the Grand Prix, the GP700, to take a child and an adult side by side.

After a lapse in production, the Wessex Sidecars manufacturing rights owned by Weymouth Components were bought by P.

J. Turner of Lyme Regis, Dorset. Although the overall shape remained unaltered, slight modifications were made. The bubble screen was increased in height and the boot was made to open from the rear. Several batches of this aerodynamic model were made during the late 1970s and the 1980s for the British market, and a small number of right-hand sidecars for export. Wessex sidecars are no longer available.

In 1988 P. Primmer began West Country Sidecars in Fordingbridge, Hampshire, with the fibre-glass Diplomat, a single-seat sports with an ample seat and large boot space. The integral mudguard includes a side spotlight, set neatly in the moulding, and a radial tyre is fitted on to the 10 inch (25 cm) wheel. A saloon in moulded fibre-glass has also been produced; called the Ambassador, it is a spacious double-adult sidecar with a hinged canopy and the wheel set within the body. West Country Sidecars also offer motorcycle trailers, mudguards and other mouldings for the sidecarrist.

Launched in 1989, the fibre-glass Crusader double-adult saloon is a touring sidecar made by Crusader Productions of Norwich. It has gull-wing doors and a sleek

Both these Wessex sports sidecars are prototypes. A number of this model were made in the 1970s and 1980s and the production model changed very little.

Right: *West Country Sidecars' second model, the Ambassador, with a forward-hinged front canopy for access to front and rear seats. A spotlight is fitted in the side and the wheel is neatly set within the body line.*

Below: *The imported Russian Neval 650 motorcycle and the military sidecar which is a copy of the German Second World War Steib military sidecar.*

wrap-around screen and the 10 inch (25 cm) wheel is set within the body. This model is more suited for the larger motorcycle.

Neval Motorcycles of Hull has been

importing the Russian Cossack 650 with military sidecar and the smaller 350 with sports sidecar since 1972. In 1974 the Jawa 350 motorcycle was first fitted with the Squire Javelin sidecar and later with the Jawa Velorex sports sidecar.

On the sporting scene, by the 1970s the road-racing outfits had changed considerably. The sidecar was now mainly a custom-made chassis under a low-profile fibre-glass moulding with integral fairing for the motorcycle. The wheelbase had lengthened, tyres were 13 by 6 inches (33 by 15 cm) on all three wheels and the engine was placed further forward to hold down the front end under acceleration. The lowered profile became known as the kneeler outfit. In the 1980s and 1990s the front leading links were improved, using hub-centre steering, the fuel tank became part of the monocoque chassis, the engine was placed at the rear, and the outfit's

Sand racing at Weston-super-Mare in Somerset The grass-track type outfit is fairly stable, providing a good platform for the passenger to move about on, and the essential hand holds

Left: *A Dutch EML motocross outfit, with leading link front forks and a wide platform for the sidecar passenger, with plenty of hand holds when standing, kneeling or leaning out over the sidecar wheel on left-hand cornering.*

Below: *This huge side-carrier, the ultimate 3 Series Clarksons Special, was made by Ross Clarkson for carrying motor factor spares. The motorcycle engine is fitted into the Trisis frame and integral chassis to form this trade vehicle.*

length and width were increased to aid stability. Trials sidecars are mostly custom-built by the enthusiasts, as are the grass-track, motocross and speedway sidecars, often incorporating Wasp suspension and leading links. Leading links and suspension units from EML in Holland are also very popular in Britain, on both touring and sporting combinations.

The Ministry of Defence has lost interest in sidecar combinations and they are rarely seen as trade carriers. Examples are in use as an outside catering vehicle and for carrying gardeners' and carpenters'

The Flexit sidecar from Watsonian Squire had an ultra-modern style and performance was unmistakable, as it could fluidly lean to left or right with the motorcycle. It accommodated one adult or two children, and the screen's supporting runners allowed as much wind protection as required.

tools, window-cleaners' ladders and buckets. Another, called the Clarksons Special, is in regular use as a sidecarrier loaded with motor factor products.

One of the new sidecars introduced in the early 1990s was the Flexit. When coupled to the motorcycle, as the name implies, the outfit will lean to either right or left, making cornering no different from solo motorcycling. The Flexit was not a new idea, however, as this concept had been used by a few firms over the years. The Flexit sidecar had its origins in South Africa and Holland and was marketed and fitted by Watsonian Squire in Gloucestershire. The passenger body with stowage space was in moulded fibre-glass and the aerodynamic body shape had a curved sliding screen on runners, which was electrically operated, moving at the touch of a button to the required position. A wide-profile tyre was fitted to the 10 inch (25 cm) disc-braked wheel, having damped suspension on either side. Because the wheel was located under the centre of the sidecar body there was no mudguard. The chassis was H-frame design with two attachments to the motorcycle, a front ball joint and a rear hinge. Meshed chains and two quadrants allowed lean to left or right. There was a locking lever, purely for very slow driving before parking the outfit. Owing to the solo-type handling of a Flexit outfit, no sidecar front leading link forks were necessary and the motorcycle retained its solo tyres. Availability of the Flexit ceased in 2001.

Another early 1990s sidecar is the Charnwood Sports Special single-seat from Charnwood Classic Restorations of Leicestershire. Made in fibre-glass, it is a moulded sleek sports with a narrow, well-shaped screen and a chassis perimeter

frame all round for protection. The medium-sized wheel is sprung by a leading link pivot arm and damped suspension. This sidecar blends very well with the modern faired-in sports motorcycle and is still being made in the twenty-first century.

Watsonian Squire produced the large child-adult RX4 Sports sidecar early in the 1990s. A spacious fibre-glass sidecar with a big opening boot, the RX4 has a conventional chassis with a medium-sized damped wheel. Although wide, it has a sleek appearance and is fitted with a large, well-angled screen.

The Grand Prix Sports from Watsonian Squire (first produced in the early 1960s) was updated in the early 1990s to a widened version, a child and adult seater, called the GP700, set within the same-style Silk chassis, but on a large wheel and with a motorcycle-type mudguard fitted. This was followed by two new Watsonian Squire sidecars, the Stratford and the GP Manx. They are both lightweights aimed at the rider of smaller motorcycles, and consequently they are available in a lower price range. The Stratford single-seat sports is the lighter in weight of the two models, on a 16 inch (41 cm) wheel with rubber-in-torsion leading link suspension. There is a rather upright screen, and a chrome bumper bar and luggage rack are optional extras. The eyecatching GP Manx, described as a new variant of the popular GP Sports, is shorter but with a higher boot shape and is fitted into a reduced version of the all-round Silk chassis. The 16 inch (41 cm) wheel suspension is hydraulically damped, with leading link arm on taper roller bearings.

Left: *Charnwood Classic Restorations have in the twenty-first century produced two more sports sidecars, the Meteor Sport, which is on a large wheel and with a modest small neat screen, and the Charnwood Royal Tourer Sport (shown here). To attract families, the Royal Tourer seats either a child and an adult or two children. The small wheel sits neatly under the integral mudguard and there is a generous screen and roll bar, plus ample boot space.*

Right: *Merlin Sidecars, a family-run business, produces touring sports sidecars, using their experience in race technology. Their first model, the Super Sport, is a single-seater with a low screen and lockable boot space and was originally launched with very distinctive 'eyes' artwork. Some thought this was a gimmick but Merlin sidecars are now serious contenders in the sidecar scene. All paintwork is done in house and customers can order the finish of their choice; a Merlin sidecar can be matched to the customer's motorcycle.*

Left: *In 2002 the Reverend Paul Sinclair of Leicestershire established Motorcycle Funerals Ltd to meet the demand for a motorcycle-orientated hearse, to provide a dignified final ride for motorcycle enthusiasts. The hearse body is a sidecar, a custom-built fibre-glass moulding, capable of carrying a full-size coffin. The rear door of the hearse hinges at the top, and there is a roof rack for floral tributes. This business now runs a fleet of sidecar hearses coupled to large-capacity motorcycles, which can operate anywhere in Britain.*

CUSTOM-MADE MOTORCYCLES FOR SIDECAR WORK

Specifically built motorcycles intended purely for sidecar work have been considered from time to time, but such a project had to be financially viable. For the majority of sidecarrists, the simple procedure of bolting the new sidecar to their existing motorcycle had to suffice.

In 1931 George Brough, a dedicated sidecar man known for the Brough Superior motorcycles, produced a motorcycle with twin rear wheels and an Austin car engine as a sidecar machine. An Austin four-cylinder four-stroke engine was fitted, of 747 cc, with a three-speed gearbox with reverse, and a self-starter. A shaft drive went to the QD (quickly detachable) twin rear wheels, which were close together, with 19 inch (48 cm) front and rear wheels. The motorcycle had a 4½ gallon (20 litre) fuel tank but the Brough Black Alpine sports sidecar, with which it could be fitted, also incorporated the Brough special large-diameter chassis loop over the sidecar nose and this acted as an

auxiliary fuel tank to feed the main fuel tank. A Schrader pressure valve was fitted at the top of the loop, situated in front of the sidecar screen. Ten of these motorcycles were sold over three years.

The Watsonian sidecar firm from Birmingham put forward their idea of the ideal sidecar machine in 1950, using a 996 cc JAP engine. This prototype had chain drive to a four-speed Burman gearbox, and the fuel tank carried over 5 gallons (23 litres), but no production models followed.

With the popularity of small three- and four-wheeled cars increasing at the expense of the combination from the late 1950s, no more specialised motorcycles were made until in 1982 Neval Motorcycles of Hull produced the Regent. Exhibited at the motorcycle show held at the National Exhibition Centre, Birmingham, this motorcycle was designed to take the Vauxhall Chevette car engine, had shaft drive, car wheels and the Regent

Watsonian chose the 996 cc V-twin JAP engine in 1950 for their prototype motorcycle. It had chain drive but no reverse gear.

The 1980s Austel Pullman, with a 1300 cc Mini car engine. It has the advantage of shaft drive with a reverse gear and it was in limited production.

leading link front forks, and was fitted with Neval's own fibre-glass sidecar, the Regent Corvette. This firm then became known as Sidecar International, as they were already importers of the Russian combinations. A number of the Regent Corvette sidecars were produced, but the Regent motorcycle never went beyond the prototype stage.

The prototype Austel motorcycle appeared in 1984, going into production in 1985. It was made by Austel Engineering in Berkshire and again a car engine was favoured, because of the availability of spares and the economic fuel consumption. The Austel Pullman had a 1300 cc Leyland Mini car engine, arranged in line, shaft-drive four-speed gearbox with reverse, 13 inch (33 cm) car wheels, Austel leading link anti-dive design front forks and a 5 gallon (23 litre) fuel tank. Production was on a limited scale.

The concept of the Trisis, introduced by Geoff Clark of Yorkshire in 1988, was a sidecar conversion using race technology. It consisted of a rolling chassis of semi-integral box-section construction to take the motorcycle engine and sidecar body of the customer's choice. The Trisis 21 standard-width and the Trisis 22 wide-track were to take the wider sidecar body or trade box. It came with hub centre steering (as used in the Reliant car), QD 14 inch (36 cm) car wheels, and chain or shaft drive. Sidecar Conversions (Trisis) began production in 1989 and guaranteed superb road-holding capabilities.

FURTHER READING

Axon, Jo. *Our Sidecars.* Jo Axon, 1988. An account of British sidecars.
Brazendale, Geoff. *The Sidecar, A History.* Geoff Brazendale, 1999.
Clew, Jeff. *Motorcycling in the 50s.* Veloce Publishing, 1995.
Franitza, Martin. *Sidecars: General.* M. Franitza, Germany, 1987. Well illustrated, with captions.
Franitza, Martin. *Sidecars: Scooters.* M. Franitza, Germany, 1988. Well illustrated, with captions.
Franitza, Martin. *Sidecars: Early.* M. Franitza, Germany, 1989. Well illustrated, with captions.
Kendall, Hal. *Sidecar Catalog.* H. Kendall, USA, not dated. International sidecar reference, illustrated.
Kendall, Hal. *Sidecar Operator.* H. Kendall, USA, not dated. Driving instruction.
Koenigsbeck, Axel. *Motorrad-Gespanne heute.* Motorbuch Verlag, Germany, 1989. Detailed technical
    sidecar coverage.
Procter, John. *Watsonian Sidecars.* J. Procter, 1987. History of Watsonian sidecars.
Rae, Ron. *The Goulding Album.* R. Rae, USA, 1990. History of the Goulding sidecar.
Santner, Rudolf. *Österreichische Motorräder und Beiwagen 1918-1960.* Herbert Weishaupt, Austria,
    1994. Well-illustrated account of Austrian motorcycles and sidecars.

PLACES TO VISIT

Practically all vehicle shows and festivals of transport include motorcycle combinations. The Federation of Sidecar Clubs holds an annual rally on August Bank Holiday at which a large variety of classic and modern outfits can be seen. For the venue contact Watsonian Squire Limited (address below).

MUSEUMS
Before travelling, intending visitors are advised to check the times of opening and also to make sure that items of particular interest will be on display.

Craven Classic Motorcycles, Brockfield Villa, Stockton on Forest, York YO1 9UE.
    Telephone: 01904 400493. Website: www.cravencollection.co.uk
Lambretta Scooter Museum, 77 Alfred Street, Weston-super-Mare, Somerset BS23 1PP.
    Telephone: 01934 614614. Website: www.scooterproducts.com
London Motorcycle Museum, Ravenor Farm, Oldfield Lane South, Greenford, Middlesex UB6 9LD
    Telephone: 0208 575 6644. Website: www.london-motorcycle-museum.co.uk
National Motorcycle Museum, Coventry Road, Bickenhill, Solihull, West Midlands B92 0EJ.
    Telephone: 01675 443311. Website: www.nationalmotorcyclemuseum.co.uk
National Motor Museum, John Montagu Building, Beaulieu, Brockenhurst, Hampshire SO42 7ZN.
    Telephone: 01590 612345. Website: www.beaulieu.co.uk
The Sammy Miller Museum, Bashley Manor, Bashley Cross Road, New Milton, Hampshire BH25 5SZ
    Telephone: 01425 620777. Website: www.sammymiller.co.uk
Science Museum, Exhibition Road, South Kensington, London SW7 2DD.
    Telephone: 0870 870 4868. Website: www.sciencemuseum.org.uk
Science Museum at Wroughton, Red Barn Gate, Wroughton Airfield, Swindon, Wiltshire SN4 9NS
    Telephone: 01793 846200. Website: www.sciencemuseum.org.uk/wroughton
Stanford Hall Motorcycle Museum, Stanford Hall, Lutterworth, Leicestershire LE17 6DH.
    Telephone: 01788 860250. Website: www.stanfordhall.co.uk

USEFUL ADDRESSES
Charnwood Classic Restorations, J & J Beswick, Unit 4L, Gelders Hall, Shepshed, Leicestershire LE67
    2FL. Telephone: 01530 832357. Website: www.charnwoodclassic.com
F2 Motorcycles Ltd, URAL and VELOREX imports. Unit 6 Burgess Farm, Middleton Cheney, Oxon.
    Telephone: 01295 712900. Website: www.f2motorcycles.ltd.uk
Merlin Sidecars, Front Street, Pity Me, Durham DH1 5DE.
    Telephone: 0191 386 6777. Website: www.merlinsidecars.co.uk
Motopodd, R. Young, 99 Tring Road, Wendover, Aylesbury, Buckinghamshire HP22 6NY.
    Website: www.motopodd.com
Motorcycle Funerals, Unit 7, Riverside Court, Westminster Industrial Estate, Measham, Swadlincote,
    Derbyshire DE12 7DS. Telephone: 01530 834616. Website: www.motorcyclefunerals.com
Unit Sidecars, Broomhill Composites Ltd, for Hedingham. Unit 4, Muchmores Farm, Blake End Road,
    Great Sailing, Essex. Telephone: 01787 461000.
Watsonian Squire Ltd, Northwick Business Centre, Blockley, near Moreton-in-Marsh, Gloucestershire
    GL56 9RF. Telephone: 01386 700907. Website: www.watsonian-squire.com
EZS Engbers Sidecar Service (Import), UK Agent – Len Tempest. Telephone: 01664 481348.